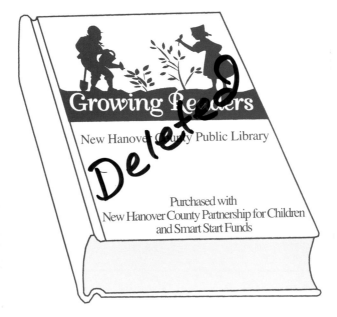

LIFE CYCLES

By Melanie Mitchell

Lerner Publications Company · Minneapolis

Look at the **rabbit**.

There are many kinds
of rabbits.

Rabbits are **mammals**, like dogs and people.

How does a rabbit grow?

Baby rabbits grow inside
their mother.

The mother rabbit makes
a **nest**.

Baby rabbits come out
of their mother.

Baby rabbits are called **kits**.

At first, kits are very small.

They have no **fur** and
cannot see.

Kits drink milk from
their mother.

Later, their eyes open and
the kits grow fur.

Young rabbits eat plants.

They learn to clean
themselves.

The young rabbits
find homes.

It is fun to watch a
rabbit grow.

Parts of a Rabbit

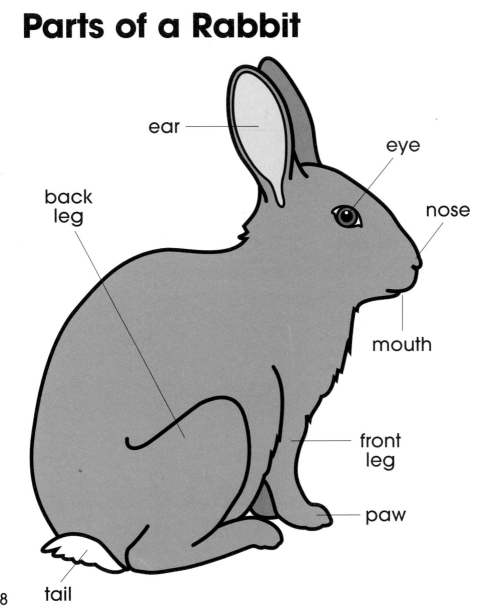

ear

eye

nose

back
leg

mouth

front
leg

paw

tail

Adult Rabbits

Adult rabbits have many different body parts. They have two short front legs and two long back legs. Their back legs help them hop. Rabbits have long ears. Their ears help them hear things far away.

Rabbits have thick fur to keep them warm. The fur of some rabbits changes color in the winter to blend in with the snow. It changes back in the spring. In the spring, rabbits get ready to have babies and begin the rabbit life cycle again.

Rabbit Fun Facts

 Many rabbits thump their back feet when they feel danger is near.

 Female rabbits are usually larger than male rabbits.

 A female rabbit is called a doe and a male rabbit is called a buck.

 Mother rabbits pull out bits of their own fur to line their nests. The fur makes the nest soft for the babies.

Cottontail rabbits live in holes called forms.

 Pet rabbits can be trained to use a litterbox just like cats.

 Rabbits have between 26 and 28 teeth.

 A rabbit's front teeth never stop growing.

Glossary

 fur – thick, soft hair covering an animal's body

 kits – baby rabbits

 mammal – a warm-blooded animal that gives birth to its young

 nest – a place for animals to raise their young

 rabbit – a mammal with long ears and soft fur

Index

drink – 12

eat – 14

fur – 11, 13, 19

kinds of rabbits – 3

kits – 9, 10, 12, 13

mammals – 4

nest – 7

The photographs in this book are reproduced through the courtesy of: © Norvia Behling, front cover, pp. 3 (top right), 4, 13, 16, 17, 22 (middle); © Dwight Kuhn, pp. 2, 6, 22 (bottom); © Art Morris/Birds as Art/Visuals Unlimited, p. 3 (bottom left); © Barbara Gerlach/Visuals Unlimited, p. 3 (bottom right); © PhotoDisc Royalty Free, p. 3 (top left); © Rob Simpson/ Visuals Unlimited, p. 5; © Bill Banaszewski/Visuals Unlimited, p. 7, 22 (second from bottom); © Gerard Fuehrer/Visuals Unlimited, p. 8; © Leonard Lee Rue III, pp. 9, 15, 22 (second from top); © Al and Linda Bristor/Visuals Unlimited, p. 10; © Lynda Richardson/CORBIS, pp. 11, 12; © Bill Beatty/Visuals Unlimited, p.14.
Illustration on p. 18 by Laura Westlund.

Lerner Publications Company
A division of Lerner Publishing Group
241 First Avenue North
Minneapolis, MN 55401 USA

Website address: www.lernerbooks.com

Library of Congress Cataloging-in-Publication Data

Mitchell, Melanie S.
    Rabbits / by Melanie Mitchell.
        p.   cm. — (First step nonfiction) (Life cycles)
    Summary: A basic overview of the life cycle of a rabbit
and the behavior of young rabbits as they grow.
    ISBN: 0–8225–4604–3 (lib. bdg. : alk. paper)
    1. Rabbits—Life cycles—Juvenile literature. [1. Rabbits.
2. Animals—Infancy.] I. Title. II. Series.
QL737.L32 M58 2003
599.32—dc21   2002003281

Manufactured in the United States of America
1 2 3 4 5 6 – JR – 08 07 06 05 04 03